Keto Cook

Simple, Nutritious & No-Nonsense Ketogenic Recipes to Burn Fat, Lose Weight and Build Muscle With Low-Carb Meals

Julia Spoon

Francis Powder

Copyright 2021 by Julia Spoon All rights reserved. This document is geared towards providing exact and reliable information in regards to the topic and issue covered. The publication is sold with the idea that the publisher is not required to render accounting, officially permitted, or otherwise, qualified services. If advice is necessary, legal or professional, a practiced individual in the profession should be ordered.
From a Declaration of Principles which was accepted and approved equally by a Committee of the American Bar Association and a Committee of Publishers and Associations.
In no way is it legal to reproduce, duplicate, or transmit any part of this document in either electronic means or in printed format. Recording of this publication is strictly prohibited and any storage of this document is not allowed unless with written permission from the publisher. All rights reserved.
The information provided herein is stated to be truthful and consistent, in that any liability, in terms of inattention or otherwise, by any usage or abuse of any policies, processes, or directions contained within is the solitary and utter responsibility of the recipient reader. Under no circumstances will any legal responsibility or blame be held against the publisher for any reparation, damages, or monetary loss due to the information herein, either directly or indirectly.
Respective authors own all copyrights not held by the publisher.
The information herein is offered for informational purposes solely, and is universal as so. The presentation of the information is without contract or any type of guarantee assurance. The trademarks that are used are without any consent, and the publication of the trademark is without permission or backing by the trademark owner. All trademarks and brands within this book are for clarifying purposes only and are the owned by the owners themselves, not affiliated with this document.

Introduction

Congratulations on purchasing *Keto Cookbook for Men,* and thank you for doing so.

The following chapters will discuss what you need to do to adopt a ketogenic diet and how easy it is to improve your life the keto way. You are about to embark on a new lifestyle because while keto is referred to as a diet, which makes referring to it more comfortable, it is not a diet but a way of life that you can follow forever. There is no diet plan that is flexible enough for anyone to live on for the remainder of their lives. Diets are meant to be restrictive, to make you give up something for the privilege of being healthy and maintaining an average weight. The keto diet is not like that. The keto lifestyle is proof you can eat good tasting food and live a healthy life.

While it is true that the keto lifestyle will restrict you from eating certain foods, it only eliminates the foods that provide nothing more than empty calories without providing you with nutritional benefits. Keto is not complicated; it is flexible and quite versatile. You will not give up good food, and you will not be hungry. And the benefits of keto are not limited to weight loss. You will also enjoy more stable moods, improved memory and mind function, and a slower aging process. Your lean muscle mass might increase...

You might have tried some of the fad diets that are all the rage right now. You might even have some weight loss success, but do you see yourself maintaining those eating plans for the remainder of your life? Weight loss and good health do not need to be complicated. You do not need to skip meals or drink your meals, and you do not need to live on bland rabbit food. You can enjoy meals with meat, green veggies, and even a dessert now and then.

There are plenty of books on this subject on the market, books that will make empty promises and leave you wanting more, so thanks again for choosing this one! Every effort was made to ensure it is full of as much useful information as possible, please enjoy!

Chapter 1: The Keto Diet

Being on a keto, diet provides all of the advantages of fasting without needing to exercise long term, including weight reduction.

When You Are in Ketosis, How Would You Know?

To figure out if you are in a ketosis condition, search for ketones in your urine. You can order ketone strips digitally or from a local pharmacy. A line that measures positive for ketones shows that you have entered a ketosis condition. Most people associate increased ketones level in the body, with a diabetic medical real crisis known as ketoacidosis. Still, there are somewhat distinct conditions, dietary ketosis involved with the keto diet and diabetic ketoacidosis.

1.1 Types of Keto Diet

These are different types of keto diets, available:

Standard keto diet: The diet (SKD) is very small in oil, mild in protein, and extra fat can be utilized. Usually, it comprises 20% protein, 75% fat and just 5 percent carbohydrates.

Targeted keto diet: The plan (TKD) of this diet allows carbohydrates to incorporate into workouts.

Cyclical keto diet: Cyclical keto diet (CKD): involves higher-carbohydrate refeed cycles such as five keto days and then two days of high-carb.

High in protein keto diet: Close to a traditional keto diet, except with extra protein. The composition is often 35% protein, 60% fat, and 5% carbohydrates.

However, scientists have conducted an extensive study of standard and high protein keto diets only. This knowledge often applies to the standard keto diet (SKD); however, many of the same instructions still apply to the other variations. Keto diet is also an important means of losing weight and does not have any disease risk factors. However, studies show that the keto diet is now far beneficial for the people than to the often-prescribed low in the fat diet plan.

The food is also so rich in nutrients; you would lose weight without calorie counting or tracking your dietary intake. One study found that people on a keto diet lost 2.1 significantly more likely than those on a low fat, calorie-limited diet and improved triglyceride and HDL cholesterol rates. Another study has found that people on the keto diet lose three relatively faster than they lose those on a diabetes UK diet. There are other reasons why a keto diet is superior to a low in the fat diet, which includes high protein intake, and has many benefits. The cause may be the reduced ketones, lower cholesterol levels, and enhanced response to insulin. A Keto diet can help you lose weight. Initially, in the first three to six months compared with certain other diets. It could be because more calories are required to transform fat into energy than to convert carbohydrates into energy. A high protein and high-fat diet are more likely to suit you more; maybe you are eating fewer, so it is not yet verified.

Keto Diet with Diabetes and Prediabetes

Diabetes is marked by shifts in appetite, increased blood pressure, and decreased regulation of insulin. The keto diet can help lose excess weight, which is closely correlated with type two diabetes, prediabetes which metabolic syndrome. Another study carried out by people with type 2 diabetes has found that 7 out of 21 participants could stop using any diabetes medications. On yet another study, the party that followed the keto diet lost 24.4 pounds (11.1 kg) in comparison to 15.2 pounds (6.9 kg) in the higher-carb band. It is a significant benefit when considering the weight-to-type two diabetes connection. By contrast, 95.2 percent of the keto community was also willing to avoid or decrease diabetes treatment, compared to 62 percent of the higher-carb community. Individuals are most inclined to try a keto diet to lose weight, and this may help cure some medical conditions, such as epilepsy. If you practice the keto diet, it can even benefit patients with heart failure, other brain conditions, and wrinkles, although further work has to be done in certain fields. First, you should talk to your doctor about whether it is okay for a person like you to go on a keto diet if you have type 1 diabetes. For starters, a keto diet may help increase strength athletes and runners and cyclists. It increases the muscle to fat ratio over time, increasing the volume of oxygen that the body can absorb when working hard. Thus, it may help in the preparation, high efficiency.

How Does It Work?

The keto diet's purpose is to use a different type of fuel in your body. Rather than focusing on carbohydrate sugar (glucose: such as rice, legumes, beans, and fruits), the keto diet is influenced by ketone bodies, a form of fuel the liver creates from fat. Burning food is an effective way to lose weight. However, making ketone bodies into the liver is tricky:

You must deprive yourself of carbohydrates, must take less than 50g of carbs each day (remember a small banana contains about more than 25g of carbs).

It typically takes several days to get to a ketosis state.

Having too much protein will hinder to get into a ketosis stage.

1.2 Keto Kitchen

What Should You Eat?

Since there is such a great fat element of the keto diet, participants will consume fat in every meal. It would be like 40g of sugars, 165g of weight, and 75g of protein in a regular 2000 calorie (food) diet. Although, the specific amount of nutrients depends on the individual requirements. The keto diet makes certain good unsaturated fats like walnuts, almonds, peas, olive oil, avocados, tofu. Yet largely saturated fats are recommended from oils like palm oil, coconut oil, lard, milk.

Meat is portion of the keto diet but it does not typically distinguish between lean protein products and high source of protein in fat like bacon and pork. Most fruits are high in carbohydrates, but you can get other fruits like blueberries in limited amounts. Vegetables (also high in carbohydrates) are restricted to greens vegetables like black bell peppers, brussels sprouts, kale, spinach, cauliflower, asparagus, mushrooms, onions, celery, garlic, cucumber, and squashes. Even a bowl of broccoli is diced and contains approximately six carbohydrates.

How Can You Follow A Keto Diet?

There are many forms of a keto diet, but you have to drastically decrease the number of carbohydrates you consume to reach a ketosis condition. (The keto tracker can be used to create a custom food plan.) Estimates suggest that the average adult man over the age of 20 absorbs 47.4 %of his daily calories from carbs. The average adult woman over the age of 20 consumes 49.6 % of her daily calories from carbs. Yet 80 to 90 % of calories come from fat, 5 to 15 % come from protein, and 5 to 10 % come from carbs in the standard keto diet, which was first intended to treat seizure disorders. The most widely practiced variation of the plan currently is a simplified form of the keto diet that encourages you to consume protein more liberally — about 20 to 30 %of the daily calories — for the remaining starch limit. Many of a keto diet's new edition goals are weight reduction, weight control, and better athletic results.

The keto diet has been changed variously. Following a keto

diet, most individuals follow the so-called traditional keto diet program, which contains approximately 10 % of the overall carbohydrate calories. Other types of keto diets include cyclic keto diets, carb cycling, and guided keto diets that require carbohydrate intake to be changed through exercise. Usually, these changes are introduced by athletes looking to use the keto diet to enhance performance and endurance rather than by focusing on weight loss. Yet broadly speaking, if you intend on adopting a keto diet, you will target eating fewer than 10 % of the total carbohydrate calories a day. The remaining calories should be 20 to 30% calcium and 60 to 80% fat. A recent study suggests that if you eat a 2,000-calorie diet regularly, no more than 200 calories (or 50 g) will come from sugars, whereas 400 to 600 calories will come from protein, and 1,200 to 1,600 from fat. (There is a reason this program is often dubbed a low-carbohydrate, high-fat diet).

Main Ingredients to Be Used in A Keto Diet

How does the keto-friendly shopping bag look like to you?

Clear all enticing carb-heavy products in your pantry and fridge. Snacks with sugar, processed foods, bread and rice, starchy vegetables, Sweeteners like jellies, honey, jams, agave nectar, and others before you start shopping. The ingredients to make up the pantry basket to make keto recipes for a keto beginner are mentioned below. We propose that you double the ingredients and proteins to cook together with our recipes at home! **Regular Keto Diet Catalog of Acceptable Foods:**

Proteins

Ingredients

- Breakfast sausage
- Boneless, skinless chicken breasts
- Bacon
- Ground beef

Produce

Ingredients

- White onion
- mushrooms
- Garlic
- Spinach
- Avocado
- Romaine or leaf lettuce
- Green cabbage
- Green onions
- Red bell black pepper
- Cherry tomatoes
- Lime

Eggs and Dairy

Ingredients

- Sea salted butter
- Plain, whole milk yogurt
- Cream cheese
- Eggs
- Blue cheese

Pantry Supplies

Ingredients

- Cocoa powder
- Chicken broth
- Coconut cream
- Monk fruit extract

- Vanilla extract
- Almond flour
- Soy sauce
- Almond butter

Oils and Spices

Ingredients

- Sea salt
- Garlic powder
- Black pepper
- Ground ginger
- Cinnamon
- Coconut oil
- Sesame seed
- Sesame oil
- Avocado oil
- Vegetables with no starch like broccoli, black peppers, mushrooms, onions, leafy greens and cauliflower, cabbage.
- Dairy, including cheese, eggs
- Protein (source) as in soybeans, fish, beef, pork, shellfish, and poultry
- Sunflower seeds, walnuts, peanuts, pistachios, and pumpkin seeds
- Fats, such as cooking oil, butter.

Foods You Should Stop During the Ketogenic Diet or Reduce It:

- Processed products such as crackers, chips of maize and packet chips
- Cookies include cookies, cakes, and brownies
- All sorts of grains, including quinoa, bread, rice, and pasta.
- Fruits are rich in carbon like tropical fruits, melons.
- Sweeteners that include Equal, Splenda.

- While both nuts and seeds are low in net carbohydrates, the sum between the various forms differs quite a bit.

Here Are the Carb Counts of Some Common Nuts and Seeds For 2 tbsp.:

- Almonds: 3 grams of carbs net (6 grams of carbs total)
- Brazilian nuts: 1-gram of carbs net (3 grams of carbs total)
- Cashews: 8 grams of carbs net (9 grams of carbs total)
- Macadamia nuts: 2 grams of carbs net (4 grams of carbs total)
- Total pecan: 1 gram of carbs net (4 grams of carbs total)
- Pistachios: 5 grams of carbs net (8 grams of carbs total)
- Walnuts: 2 grams of carbs net (4 grams of carbs total)
- Chia seeds: 1-gram of carbs net (12 grams of carbs total)
- Flaxseeds: 0 grams of carbs net (8 grams of carbs total)
- Pumpkin seeds: 4 grams of carbs net (5 grams of carbs total)
- Sesame seeds 3 grams of carbs net (7 grams of carbs total)

Here are the carb counts of certain berries for 7 tbsp. (100 grams)

- Blackberries: 5 grams of carbs net (10 grams of carbs total)
- Blueberries: 14 grams of carbs net (12 grams of carbs total)
- Raspberries: 6 grams of carbs net (12 grams of carbs total)
- Strawberries: 6 grams of carbs net (8 grams of carbs total)

Chapter 2: The Benefits of Keto for Men

The keto diet is an eating lifestyle that focuses on consuming a higher amount of fat than protein and minimal carbohydrates. Replacing your carbs with higher fat content will put your body into ketosis, and this is the optimal state for your body to lose weight and feel great. When your body enters ketosis, it creates ketones from the fat it burns for energy, so the diet got its name. Instead of relying on the sugar from digested carbs and processed foods, your body will burn fat to create ketones for energy. Following the keto diet will provide your body with many benefits.

Weight Loss

Whether you need to lose a few pounds or half your body weight, the keto diet will allow you to attain the weight loss goals you set for yourself. Losing weight will give you so many more benefits than just a leaner physique. Carrying excess body weight will make you prone to developing many other chronic health problems. It is estimated that most chronic health problems are caused, at least in part, by being overweight. The overweight person consumes too much food, and they likely consume a diet based on processed foods, sugar, and saturated fats. Even if you are not overweight, continuously consuming a diet lacking proper nutrition can lead to inflammation, arthritis, skin irritations, gallbladder disease, and cardiovascular system diseases. You will not need to starve yourself to reduce all your health risks. You will fill yourself with good fats and proteins to keep you feeling full while helping you lose weight.

Increased Energy

The ketones produced by the keto diet are responsible for increasing your energy levels for several reasons. By themselves, they are a powerful source of energy. Ketones are superior to glucose when providing power for your body. The low carb feature of the keto diet means you will not subject your body to the peaks and crashes caused by metabolizing carbs and sugary foods. Your energy levels will remain constant and more substantial since you are not using energy to keep your systems functioning steadily. And fat is a slower digesting food than carbs so that it will feed your energy levels longer and more steadily. Losing excess weight will also increase your energy levels since you will find it easier to move, and movement creates energy. High-calorie meals, especially those loaded with processed foods and carbs, tend to make you sleepy and lethargic. The keto diet makes you feel energetic and alert.

Better Concentration

Your brain will use ketones to power its functions just as quickly as it will use glucose, and you will find the brain functions better on the keto diet. Besides consuming foods that help you feel energetic and alert, the keto diet will benefit your brain in numerous ways. The plaque that forms on a standard Western diet, clogging your arteries and diminishing your brain function, will be eliminated on the keto diet. While your brain is small compared to the rest of your body, it is the organ that uses the most energy of all the organs in your body. A diet high in carbs and processed foods will flood your brain with glucose and lead to brain fog—the ketones produced by the keto diet fuel your brain without causing fog and other disruptions.

Heart Health

People who are overweight increase their risk of developing heart disease. Even people who are not overweight but frequently consume saturated fats and sugary foods are at higher risk of many chronic illnesses. Excess weight and poor dietary habits make your heart work harder, builds plaque in your arteries, and elevates your cholesterol, blood sugar, and blood pressure. Following the keto diet will help you eliminate the risk factors for heart disease.

Decreased Inflammation

Inflammation is the primary cause of most chronic illnesses. While you are following the keto diet to eliminate excess weight and improve your resistance to chronic diseases, you will be lowering or eliminating inflammation levels in your body. Reducing inflammation will also help you feel more energetic.

Increased Testosterone Levels

There is the cholesterol level your doctor measures as part of your health exam, and there is dietary cholesterol. The latter is a natural part of the foods you eat, particularly in many foods allowed on the keto diet. You consume dietary cholesterol when you eat eggs, chicken, beef, butter, and seafood. Your body will use this dietary cholesterol to create higher levels of testosterone. This hormone will help you burn fat and develop and maintain muscle mass.

On the keto diet, you will reduce your appetite, which will cause you to lose weight without starving yourself. Your bad cholesterol will decrease as good cholesterol increases. Your blood pressure will lower, and your blood sugar levels will stabilize. You will experience an increase in the powers of your memory and your brain function. No other lifestyle will give you the health benefits of the keto diet as it reduces the unhealthy factors in your life, replacing them with vitality and good health.

Chapter 3: Basic Cooking Terminology

You might be a novice to cooking your food, or you may have been cooking all your life. If cooking is a novel experience for you, it will help you know what some of the cooking terms will see. And even if you have been cooking for ages, there might be one or two terms that you don't quite understand. Knowing what these words mean might make the difference between creating a great dish and creating an inedible product.

Al dente – this term you might be familiar with if you cook pasta regularly, but this term also applies to cooking veggies. Foods that are cooked this way will still be a bit chewy when you bite into them so that the food will be somewhat firm and not soggy.

Bake or roast – both of these terms involve using the oven, and they are similar in their meaning. Roasting implies that the food item is cooked in the oven while dry to roast meat or veggies. Baking is also done in the range, but this term usually applies to casseroles and dishes similar to quiches and frittatas.

Broil or grill – these are two more terms that are similar in their meaning. They both involve cooking food uncovered using a heat source near the food. But broiling is done in the broiler part of the oven, and grilling implies using an outdoor cooking method.

Cream – you will cream (blend well) items like butter or heavy whipping cream.

Brown, sear, and sauté – these cooking methods are all similar. When you sauté your food, you will cook it in fat or oil over high heat, continually stirring while the food cooks. Chinese stir fry is a sautéed food. Brown and sear are similar. To brown the food, which is usually meat, means to cook it until the outside is brown. The sear goes a step beyond brown and is done over high heat with no oil in the skillet. The purpose of searing is to lock the flavor in the meat. Searing can be done before the meat is cooked using another method. Reverse searing is done to add a crust to the piece of meat after it is cooked using another way.

Fillet – this refers to a cooking method and a cut of meat or fish. A filet has no bones, so if you filet a piece of meat or fish, you remove the bones before cooking.

Season to taste, or a dash or pinch – some recipes will tell you exactly how much seasoning to use, and some will let you decide how much to use. If you season to taste, you will do precisely that—season the food until the taste suits your palate. You might bury your steak in black pepper, but that is your choice. A dash measures to about one-eighth of a teaspoon, and a pinch is about half of that. You can also measure a pinch by actually pinching the seasoning between your thumb and forefinger.

Fold – this cooking technique is essential when you are working with items like egg whites, heavy whipping cream, or mixing dry ingredients into wet ingredients. When you 'fold,' you will place your spatula or spoon under the ingredients at the bottom of the bowl and gently bring them up to cover the elements you just added to the bowl. So if you are adding heavy whipping cream to a recipe, you will place the cream on top of the dry or moist ingredients in the bowl and then gently scoop some of those ingredients up to cover the whipping cream. You will continue to gently do this until all of the whipping cream is incorporated into the other components, and then stop.

Simmer and boil – both of these techniques involve liquid and a pot on the stove. When you turn on the heat under the liquid, it will begin to warm, and eventually, small bubbles will appear on the bottom of the pot and rise to the top. This is called a simmer. When the bubbles become large and more frequent, the liquid is boiling. If the bubbles are rolling over one another, you have created a rolling boil.

Mince, dice, chop, and slice – other than a slice, many people use these words interchangeably even though they mean different things. A slice is a slice, where you start with the knife at the top of the food item and push or saw the blade down through the food item to cut off a slice. The other three use the same technique, and the difference is in the size of the completed product. Chop is the largest size, where you chop a food item into chunks at least a half-inch long. When you dice, you will cut the food into the same fragments, but they will be closer to one-fourth inch long. And when you mince your food, you will make the pieces tiny, making them look almost like large grains of sand. The difference in the technique refers to what you intend to do with the food. Chopping an onion is appropriate to make kabobs, dicing would be better for a stir fry, and you would mince the onion to add it to your scrambled eggs.

Herbs and spices – yes, these are different. Spice is usually a finely ground version of an herb. An herb is the leafy or green part of the plant used for flavoring or seasoning a recipe. Herbs can be used fresh or dried. Spices are the dried part of the plant that has been pulverized for your use. Spices are made from seeds, berries, roots, and bark.

Zest – this is the rind of a citrus fruit that is grated and added to recipes for flavor.

Butterfly – this technique refers to slicing almost through the center of a thick piece of meat, like a chicken breast or pork chop, to expose more flesh to the cooking process.

Grease – this means to rub some fat on the bottom and insides of a baking dish to keep the food from sticking to the dish while cooking. In keto cooking, you will use lard or butter.

Degrees of doneness – chicken, fish, and pork need to be thoroughly cooked and reach the appropriate internal temperature, but beef can be cooked to various degrees and still be safe to eat. The only exception is ground beef, which should always be cooked thoroughly to avoid foodborne illness. Rare meat is soft and has a red center, and it will probably still bleed a bit. Medium rare is slightly firmer, and the center is still red, but the center will be warm and not cold. Medium meat is firm, and the center is pink, not red. Medium well gives you just a tiny strip of pink in the center of the cut of meat. Well-done meat will be firm and utterly grayish with no red or pink visible.

You do not need to be a master chef to prepare delicious food, and you need to know what all the words mean. With regular practice, you will soon be cooking like a professional.

Chapter 4: Keto Kitchen Equipment

It is entirely possible to begin living the keto lifestyle with the cooking utensils you currently have in your kitchen. Good food can easily be prepared with just a few pieces of cookware. But as you delve deeper into the keto lifestyle, you might want to add different components to your current lineup of items. Some of these items are necessary, and some are nice to have, and all of them will make your life in the kitchen easier, helping you prepare those delicious meals you are already considering.

Kitchen knives – a good set of knives is mandatory for every kitchen so that you can invest in a good group. You can buy a set of knives in an attractive block, or you can buy the three knives mandatory for every kitchen: a chef's knife, paring knife, and serrated knife. The paring knife is used to dice and chop foods. You can also use it for slicing smaller foods. A serrated knife is used for cutting any food item with a soft center, like a tomato, which usually squashes flat when sliced with a blade that is not serrated. A chef's knife is also called a butcher knife, and you will use it for most of your kitchen cutting needs. It is best to go to a store and feel the blades before you buy them. Since a paring knife is small, you need to make sure it does not get lost in your hand. The handle of the chef's knife needs to be comfortable for you to hold. The blade should feel balanced, not too light but not too heavy.

Spatula – you will want several of these in different sizes for different uses. The spatula with the straight handle and the silicone top is used for mixing recipes and scooping ingredients out of a bowl. This spatula is also used for folding ingredients when mixing. The spatula with the more extended bent handle and the flat part on end is used for cooking, and the flat part will come in different sizes, which makes flipping other sized food easier. While you can use a smaller one on a hamburger patty, it might not do well when flipping a pancake. Whether these are metal or plastic depends on your cookware. If you use cast iron cookware, you can safely use a metal utensil, but all other cookware requires a plastic utensil.

Cutting board – unless you have a kitchen counter that is safe for slicing meat and chopping lettuce, you will need one or more cutting boards. These come in plastic-style materials and various types of wood. The plastic ones will work well for years for slicing meats and chopping veggies. They will dull your knives with continued use, they can develop little cuts and grooves that may hold bacteria if the board is not sanitized regularly, and they aren't beautiful. Wooden panels, usually made from bamboo or butcher block, look better and don't beat up your knives. Wooden cutting boards can't be washed in the dishwasher for easy germ killing. You might want to choose one wooden and one plastic cutting board for different uses. Look for extra features like a grove surrounding the board near the outside to catch juices, a handle for carrying, and ones that are not too heavy. Wooden cutting boards can also be used for serving.

Mixing bowls – you will need mixing bowls in various sizes to create your delicious keto concoctions. They are made in plastic, glass, or ceramic. Some have measurements marked on the side or come with lids. Glass bowls wash quickly and do not pick up stains from the food they hold. You can purchase three, four, or five bowls together as a set. Like the cutting board, a mixing bowl can be used for serving.

Colander and strainer – these are two different utensils that do the same job. A colander looks like a plastic mixing bowl with drain holes in the bottom, and it usually has a small handle on either side. A strainer is made from delicate mesh and looks like a small bowl on the end of a handle that is about six to eight inches long. While both items will drain liquid, a colander works best for larger quantities of food, while a strainer is excellent for separating egg yolks from egg whites.

Tongs – these need no explanation as to their appearance or use. They are invaluable for turning small meats and serving them. Short ones are best for serving olives or pickles, while longer ones are used in cooking.

Thermometer – unless you want to take the chance on your meat being properly cooked, you will purchase a digital thermometer for testing the internal temperature of the meat you are cooking.

Skillets, pots, and pans – you will need something to cook your food. Pots and pans generally mean the same thing, a container of varying depth with one or two handles. A skillet is shallow and will also have one or two handles. If you use non-stick cookware, you can use less oil or fat, but these are widely used on the keto diet. You can use cast iron skillets, and these are useful for cooktop or oven cooking. Non-stick cookware is easier to clean than cast iron, but it will also wear out more quickly. And if you use non-stick cookware, all your utensils will need plastic, silicone, or wood.

Baking dishes and sheet pans – a sheet pan is also called a cookie sheet or a baking sheet. You will need one of these and a few baking dishes of different sizes. These come in glass or metal, eight inches or nine inches square, nine by thirteen inches, or eleven by seventeen inches. Buy the minimum that you need initially, and you can always add on more pieces as you feel you need them. You might also want to purchase a muffin pan for making egg muffins.

Can opener – you will need a method for opening cans, and these come in manual or electric models and are very inexpensive.

Other utensils – you will need spoons for stirring, both slotted for draining and solid. One or two whisks for blending ingredients are excellent, and they come in sizes from small to extra-large.

Measuring spoons and cups – you will need these every time you create something in the kitchen to measure precise levels of the ingredients you are adding to your recipes. The spoons are made from plastic or metal, and the cups from glass, plastic, or metal. Metal or glass is easier to clean and lasts longer, but plastic is less expensive.

Towels and oven mitts – kitchen towels are used for more than decoration, and you will need something to have between your hand and the hot utensil you are reaching for.

All of the items listed above are nearly mandatory for regular cooking. The following items are nice to have, so they are unnecessary, but they will make your menu planning more exciting and give you added options for cooking.

Blender – you will want some blender for mixing sauces and dressings if you intend to make your own. This appliance can be in the form of a full-size standing blender, a small personal blender, or an immersion stick blender.

Silicone baking mats – these are formed sheets of silicone that you lay on baking sheets or baking dishes, eliminating the need for foil, parchment paper, or grease. These sheets can be used for years will careful cleaning and storage.

Masher – also known as a potato masher, this is an excellent kitchen utensil to have. While you won't be mashing potatoes with it, you can use it to mash an avocado, and it is ideal for mashing hardboiled eggs for egg salad or deviled eggs.

Countertop grill – these are wonderful for grilling meats indoors when the weather is terrible outside or for broiling meat without heating the kitchen while using the broiler in the oven.

Slow cooker – there are still stews and soups you can have on the keto diet, and the slow cooker is excellent for cooking these. It is also suitable for preparing large quantities of meat to prepare meals for many days.

Waffle maker – these are recipes for keto waffles that you can enjoy. The waffle maker is also great for making chaffles, waffle shapes made from shredded cheese. Chaffles can be used as pizza crusts or in place of bread for a sandwich.

Broiler pan – a broiler pan is excellent for broiling meats to give them a nice crusty exterior. A broiler pan is a metal baking pan with a slotted lid that sets on top. The slots allow the meat's juices to drip down into the pan and away from the meat. You will only use this pan when you broil meat, but they are not expensive and will last for years.

Trivet – these can often be found in second-hand stores. You use them to set hot dishes on the countertop or the table for serving. You can use cloth pot holders, but wooden or tile ones look much more sociable and will last longer.

Splatter guard – this is a flat piece of fine mesh screen shaped like a square or circle, with a handle attached. You lay the splatter screen over a skillet when you are frying foods to keep the food from splattering out of the skillet.

Storage containers – you really can store excess food in your mixing bowls, but you will also want storage containers. As you become more comfortable with keto cooking, you will want to make meals for several days to freeze or refrigerate. These mini-meals can go with you to work or school.

These items will allow you to have a fully functioning kitchen. If you are not opposed to used items, you can shop thrift stores and garage sales and possibly find a few bargains. Friends and family might have extra sets they would be happy to share. If you need to purchase your items, do not buy the most expensive products available, but do take the time to examine the item, like measuring spoons and bowls, so you buy something with quality. If you are purchasing an appliance or cookware, do some researches to find the best options for the amount of money you have available.

Chapter 4: One Week Keto Shopping List

Everyone has their specific food likes and dislikes, so this shopping list suggests what you can purchase to create a weeks' worth of keto eating. This list is written to have some variety, so only purchase foods you will eat. Buying this list will give you enough food to make meals for one week. Some of these items will not be purchased every week since salt and pepper will last for longer than one week. Most of the spices you use will only need to be purchased once a month, depending on how much you use.

Items with weekly replenishment needed:

- Eggs, one or two dozen
- Broccoli, one-half to one head
- Heavy whipping cream
- Cauliflower, one head
- Sour cream
- Lettuce, one or two heads
- Butter
- Spinach, fresh or frozen
- Cheddar cheese, shredded or block
- Avocado, two or three
- Grated parmesan cheese
- Lemons/Limes, two or three
- Bacon, one or two packages
- Pork rinds, one or two bags
- Ground beef, one or two pounds
- Fish, two or three servings

- Beef, two or three servings
- Pork, one or two servings
- Berries, fresh or frozen
- Arugula, one or two bunches
- Celery, one bunch
- Canned tuna or salmon, several
- Onions
- Mushrooms

Items with occasional replenishment needed:

- Olive or avocado oil
- Dijon mustard
- Mayonnaise, full
- Fatunsweetened cocoa powder
- Reduced sugar
- Ketchup, if desired
- Baking powder
- Baking soda
- Vanilla extract
- Peanut or nut butter
- Onion powder
- Canned mushrooms
- Garlic powder
- Salt
- Pepper
- Dried chives
- dried dill
- Dried basil
- Dried parsley
- Red chili flakes, if desired
- Ground cinnamon
- Ground nutmeg
- Ground ginger
- Ground turmeric
- Aluminum foil
- Parchment paper
- Soy sauce

Other herbs and spices as desired

Chapter 6: Recipes

You can experiment with different keto recipes and understand all of the delicious menus you will be consuming on the keto diet. These recipes are easy for anyone to replicate but tasty enough to share with others

6.1 Breakfast Recipes

When you are making the perfect keto breakfast, bacon and eggs are always appropriate. There are also other breakfast options, with additional ingredients, that you can create and enjoy.

Keto Loaf Bread

Total Prep & Cooking Time: 1 hour

Yields: 12 servings

Nutrition facts: Calories 239/Protein 8g/Carbs 4g/Fat 22g/Fiber 2g

Estimated cost: $10

Ingredients:

- Finely ground almond flour, 2 cups
- Baking powder, 1 teaspoon
- Coconut oil, 2 tablespoons melted and cooled
- Xantham gum, ½ teaspoon
- Butter, 1 stick softened to room temperature
- Salt, ½ teaspoon
- Eggs, 7 at room temperature

Method:

1. Heat the oven to 350 F and set the rack to the middle.

2. Grease a regular-sized loaf pan.
3. Mix the baking powder, almond flour, xanthan gum, and salt in a mixing bowl.
4. Cream together the coconut oil, melted butter, and eggs.
5. Put in the flour mixture and gently mix all ingredients.
6. Bake the mixture in the loaf pan for forty-five minutes.
7. Put the loaf on a wire rack after cooling for ten minutes in the pan after baking.

Sausage and Veggie Hash

Total Prep & Cook Time: 30 minutes
Yields: 2 servings
Nutrition facts: Calories 391/Protein 13g/Carbs 10g/Fat 34g/Fiber 2g
Estimated cost: $5

Ingredients:

- Minced garlic, 1 tablespoon
- Small turnips, 3 chopped
- Butter, 2 tablespoons
- Dried parsley, 1 tablespoon
- Olive oil, 2 tablespoons
- Small radishes, 4 chopped
- Eggs, 4
- Pepper and salt as needed

Method:

1. Boil the turnip cubes in water with two teaspoons of salt for five minutes, then drain.
2. Boil the radishes for two minutes in the same water and remove.
3. Fry the turnips and radishes in hot olive oil for seven to eight minutes, when they begin to brown.
4. Stir in the garlic and push the veggies out to make space in the mixture.
5. Melt the butter in the empty circle and add the eggs.
6. Cook the eggs until they are done to your preference.
7. Sprinkle on the dried parsley over the top and use pepper and salt as needed.

Taco Skillet

Total Prep & Cook Time: 1 hour
Yields: 6 servings
Nutrition facts: Calories 563/Protein 32g/Carbs 9g/Fat 44g/Fiber 4g
Estimated cost: $11

Ingredients:

- Ground beef, 1 pound
- Sliced green onions, 2
- Taco seasoning of choice, 4 tablespoons
- Water, 2/3 cup
- Salsa, ¼ cup
- Eggs, 10 large
- Shredded sharp cheddar cheese, 1 ½ cups divided
- Sour cream, ¼ cup
- Heavy cream, ¼ cup
- Roma tomato, 1 diced
- Avocado, 1 peeled, pitted, and cubed
- Sliced black olives, ¼ cup
- Sliced jalapeno, 1 (optional)
- Fresh cilantro, chopped, 2 tablespoons

Method:

1. Heat your oven to 375 F.
2. Cook the meat until browned and drain.
3. Set the beef back in the skillet and stir in the water and taco seasoning, simmering for 5 minutes.
4. Take half of the beef out and set it off to the side.
5. Beat the eggs together with the heavy cream and stir in 1 cup of the shredded cheese.
6. Pour the egg mixture in the beef left in the skillet and mix well.

7. If you are not using a cast-iron skillet, pour the mixture from the skillet into an 8-inch greased baking dish.
8. Bake this thirty minutes.
9. Cover the mixture with the leftover ground beef and the leftover shredded cheese, salsa, sour cream, green onion, olives, avocado, and tomato.
10. If using jalapeno and cilantro, sprinkle them on top as garnish.

Sausage Sandwich

Total Prep & Cook Time: 20 minutes

Yields: 1 serving

Nutrition facts: Calories 603/Protein 22g/Carbs 7g/Fat 54g/Fiber 3g

Estimated cost: $4.50

Ingredients:

- Sausage patties, 2
- Egg, 1
- Cream cheese, 1 tablespoon
- Salt and pepper as wanted
- Shredded sharp cheddar cheese, 2 tablespoons
- Sriracha, to taste
- Avocado, 1 peeled and sliced

Method:

1. Use the package directions to cook the sausage.
2. Blend the shredded cheddar and the cream cheese, and then microwave this for 20 to 30 seconds, just until the cheese is melted.
3. Blend the sriracha (if desired) in the cheese mixture.
4. Fry the slightly whipped egg and season as wanted.
5. Put the fried egg and the cheese mixture between the two sausage patties and enjoy.

Pulled Pork Breakfast Hash

Total Prep & Cook Time: 20 minutes
Yields: 2 servings
Nutrition facts: Calories 291/Protein 16g/Carbs 11g/Fat 21g/Fiber 3g
Estimated cost: $6.65

Ingredients:

- Avocado oil, 2 tablespoons
- Turnip, 1 diced
- Eggs, 2 large
- Paprika, ½ teaspoon
- Pulled pork, ½ cup
- Salt, ¼ teaspoon
- Diced red onion, 2 tablespoons
- Garlic powder, ¼ teaspoon
- Chopped kale, 1 cup
- Black pepper, ¼ teaspoon
- Brussels sprouts, 3 sliced in half

Method:

1. Fry the diced turnip with the spices for five minutes.
2. Stir in the rest of the veggies and fry for 3 to 4 minutes.
3. Blend in the pulled pork and fry for 2 minutes.
4. Spread the hash out to make two wells in the mixture, and then crack one egg into each well.
5. Cover the skillet, cook the eggs for four to seven minutes, or wait until they are done to your preference.

Sausage and Pepper Bake

Total Prep & Cook Time: 50 minutes
Yields: 4 servings
Nutrition facts: Calories 246/Protein 26g/Carbs 5g/Fat 13g/Fiber 1g
Estimated cost: $7.50

Ingredients:

- Grated mozzarella cheese, ½ cup
- Green bell pepper, 1 chopped
- Smoked sausage any style, 10 ounces
- Red bell pepper, 1 chopped
- Olive oil, 2 tablespoons
- Salt and pepper as needed

Method:

1. Heat your oven to 450 F.
2. Grease a nine-inch baking dish
3. Toss the chopped bell peppers with half the olive oil, set them in the baking dish, and then season.
4. Bake the bell peppers for 20 minutes.
5. While the peppers are baking, cut the sausage into chunks and fry them in the other tablespoon of the olive oil for ten minutes, stirring often.
6. Add the sausage to the bell peppers in the baking dish and sprinkle on the grated cheese.
7. Bake this dish for five more minutes.

Blueberry Pancakes

Total Prep & Cook Time: 10 minutes
Yields: 3 servings
Nutrition facts: Calories 132/Protein 7g/Carbs 4g/Fats 7g/Fiber 2g
Estimated cost: $4.75

Ingredients:

- Olive oil, 2 tablespoons
- Almond flour, ½ cup
- Blueberries, ¼ cup fresh or thawed frozen
- Coconut Flour, 2 tablespoons
- Almond milk, ¼ cup
- Ground cinnamon, 1 teaspoon
- Eggs, 3 large
- Baking powder, ½ teaspoon
- Granulated sweetener, 2 tablespoons

Method:

1. Mix the two flours with the cinnamon, sweetener, and baking powder until well mixed.
2. Add in the slightly beaten eggs and the almond milk and fold all the ingredients together.
3. Fold the blueberries in gently, just until they are blended.
4. Fry the pancakes in the olive oil, using ¼ cup of batter for each pancake, cooking each one for 3 to 4 minutes on each side.

Fresh Spinach Frittata

Total Prep & Cook Time: 45 minutes
Yields: 4 servings
Nutrition facts: Calories 661/Protein 27g/Carbs 4g/Fat 59 g/Fiber 6g
Estimated cost: $7.25

Ingredients:

- Bacon, 6 slices
- Butter, 2 tablespoons
- Dried rosemary, ½ teaspoon
- Chopped fresh spinach, 1 cup
- Black pepper, 1 teaspoon
- Eggs, 8 large
- Shredded cheddar or mozzarella cheese, ½ cup
- Heavy whipping cream, 1 cup
- Salt, ½ teaspoon

Method:

1. Heat your oven to 350 F.
2. Use grease on a nine-inch baking dish.
3. Fry the bacon in 1 tablespoon of the butter until it is crispy.
4. Add the spinach to the skillet and fry for 5 minutes, stirring to crumble the bacon.
5. Beat the eggs with the whipping cream in a mixing bowl, and then put this into the baking dish.
6. Add the bacon spinach mixture to the egg mixture.
7. Lay the shredded cheese on top and bake for 30 minutes.

Mushroom Omelet

Total Prep & Cook Time: 15 minutes

Nutrition facts: Calories 510/Protein 25g/Carbs 4g/Fat 43g/Fiber 5g

Estimated cost: $4.75

Ingredients:

- Eggs, 3
- Butter, 1 tablespoon
- Shredded cheddar cheese, ¼ cup
- Diced yellow onion, ¼ cup
- Chopped mushrooms, ¼ cup
- Salt, ½ teaspoon
- Black pepper, ½ teaspoon

Method:

1. Whip the eggs with the salt and pepper until they are slightly foamy.
2. Pour the eggs into the melted butter in a skillet.
3. Let the eggs cook undisturbed for 3 to 4 minutes until the outer edges begin to look dry.
4. Add the shredded cheese, onions, and mushrooms onto the omelet, keeping them in the middle half.
5. Fold the omelet in half and cook it for three more minutes on each side.

Ham and Egg Muffins

Total Prep & Cook Time: 30 minutes

Yields: 12 muffins

Nutrition facts: Calories 336/Protein 23g/Carbs 2g/Fat 26g/Fiber 7g

Estimated cost: $7.75

Ingredients:

- Eggs, 12
- Scallions, 2 minced
- Ham, diced, ½ cup
- Shredded cheddar cheese, ¾ cup
- Green or red pesto, 2 tablespoons
- Black pepper, ½ teaspoon
- Salt, ¼ teaspoon

Method:

1. Heat your oven to 350 F.
2. Set paper baking cups in all 12 cups of a muffin pan, then spray oil the papers lightly.
3. Add diced ham and minced scallion to the bottom of each paper cup.
4. Lightly beat the eggs.
5. Put in the salt, pepper, pesto, and shredded cheese and blend well.
6. Divide the egg mixture evenly in the paper cups.
7. Bake the egg muffins for 20 minutes.

6.2 Lunch Recipes

Shrimp Avocado Salad

Total Prep & Cook Time: 15 minutes
Yields: 4 servings
Nutrition facts: Calories255/Protein 27g/Carbs 4g/Fat 13g/Fiber 8g
Estimated cost: $6.25

Ingredients:

- Lime juice, ¼ cup
- Salt, ½ teaspoon
- Roma tomato, 1 diced
- Freshly chopped cilantro, 2 tablespoons
- Avocado, 1 peeled and diced
- Olive oil, 1 teaspoon
- Black pepper, ½ teaspoon
- Diced red onion, ¼ cup
- Small shrimp, 1 pound pre-cooked, peeled, and deveined

Method:

1. Blend the lime juice, salt, pepper, and olive oil.
2. Put the cilantro, avocado, tomato, and red onion with the shrimp and mix.
3. Pour the lime juice dressing over the shrimp, tossing gently to coat the shrimp mixture with the sauce.
4. Serve cold.

Spicy Cheesy Meatballs

Total Prep & Cook Time: 35 minutes
Yields: 12 meatballs/4 servings
Nutrition facts: Calories 660/Protein 42g/Carbs 1g/Fat 53g/Fiber 2g
Estimated cost: $9.75

Ingredients:

- Dijon mustard, 1 tablespoon
- Pimientos, ¼ cup
- Cayenne pepper, ¼ teaspoon
- Chili powder, ¼ teaspoon
- Mayonnaise, 1/3 cup
- Paprika, 1 teaspoon
- Grated cheddar cheese, ½ cup
- Black pepper, 1 teaspoon
- Salt, ½ teaspoon
- Ground beef, 2 pounds
- Butter for frying, 3 tablespoons

Method:

1. In a mixing bowl, blend the grated cheddar cheese, paprika, chili powder, cayenne pepper, mayonnaise, Dijon mustard, and pimientos and let this mixture rest for 10 minutes.
2. Blend in the pepper, salt, meat, and egg to the cheese mixture.
3. Form the mixture into 12 meatballs of equal size.
4. Fry the meatballs in the melted butter for 10 minutes, turning them often to cook on all sides.
5. Serve the meatballs with a leafy green salad.

Tuna Salad Stuffed Tomatoes

Total Prep & Cook Time: 15 minutes

Yields: 1 serving

Nutrition facts: Calories 175/Protein 15g/Carbs 8g/Fat 6g/Fiber 9g

Estimated cost: $3.85

Ingredients:

- Shredded mozzarella cheese, 1 tablespoon
- Tuna, one small can pack in oil and drained
- Fresh chopped basil, 1 tablespoon
- Tomato, 1 large
- Minced green onion, 1 tablespoon
- Balsamic vinegar, 2 teaspoons

Method:

1. Cut the core from the tomato.
2. Cut the tomato in two around the middle and scoop out half of the inside.
3. Dice the removed tomato flesh and add it to a mixing bowl.
4. Blend the green onion, tuna, shredded mozzarella, and balsamic vinegar with the diced tomato.
5. Spoon the mixture back into the tomato halves and sprinkle the fresh basil on top.

Sloppy Joes

Total Prep & Cook Time: 40 minutes
Yields: 4 servings
Nutrition facts: Calories 340/Protein 36g/Carbs 5g/Fat 8g/Fiber 2g
Estimated cost: $6.35

Ingredients:

- Yellow onion, 1 diced
- Minced garlic, 2 tablespoons
- Ground beef, 1 pound
- Celery, 1 stalk minced
- Tomato paste, ¼ cup
- Salt, ½ teaspoon
- Black pepper, 1 teaspoon
- Beef broth, ¾ cup
- Worcestershire sauce, 2 teaspoons

Method:

1. Fry the ground beef in a dry skillet, breaking it into small pieces as it cooks, for 10 minutes.
2. Drain the cooked meat and then put it back into the skillet.
3. Stir in the veggies and cook this mixture for five more minutes.
4. Blend in the salt, pepper, Worcestershire sauce, broth, and tomato paste and stir until mixed well.
5. Simmer this mixture for 20 minutes, occasionally stirring while it thickens.
6. Serve the mixture on lettuce leaves.

Chicken with Cabbage and Onion

Total Prep & Cook Time: 15 minutes
Yields: 2 servings
Nutrition facts: Calories 450/Protein 48g/Carbs 7g/Fat 22g/Fiber 11g
Estimated cost: $4.85

Ingredients:

- Dried rosemary, ½ teaspoon
- Cooked chicken, 2 cups
- Olive oil, 1 tablespoon
- Salt, ½ teaspoon
- Red onion, thinly sliced, ¼ cup
- Chopped green cabbage, 1 cup
- Greek yogurt, ½ cup
- Black pepper, ½ teaspoon

Method:

1. Set out two serving plates and divide the shredded cabbage evenly between the two.
2. Divide the onion slices and place them on top of the shredded cabbage.
3. Season this with olive oil, pepper, and salt.
4. Place a scoop of the Greek yogurt on each plate.
5. Divide the cooked chicken evenly between the two plates.
6. Sprinkle the dried rosemary over everything.

Curry and Coconut Thai Fish

Total Prep & Cook Time: 35 minutes
Yields: 4 servings
Nutrition facts: Calories 580/Protein 32g/Carbs 9g/Fat 25g/Fiber 5g
Estimated cost: $9.35

Ingredients:

- Cauliflower florets, two cups
- Dried cilantro, ½ cup
- Coconut cream, 1 cup
- Green curry paste, 2 tablespoons
- Salt, ½ teaspoon
- Black pepper, ½ teaspoon
- Turmeric, 1 teaspoon
- Curry powder, ¼ teaspoon
- Butter, 4 tablespoons
- Whitefish, 2 pounds sliced into small pieces

Method:

1. Heat your oven to 400 F.
2. Grease a rectangular baking dish.
3. Lay the fish pieces in the baking dish.
4. Put chunks of butter on top of the fish.
5. Blend the coconut cream, salt, pepper, curry powder, turmeric, cilantro, and curry paste until it is smooth.
6. Pour the coconut cream slowly over the fish pieces.
7. Bake the fish for 20 minutes.
8. While the fish is baking, boil the cauliflower florets for 5 minutes.

Southwestern Stuffed Zucchini

Total Prep & Cook Time: 45 minutes
Yields: 4 servings
Nutritional facts: Calories 601/Protein 33g/Carbs 6g/Fat 49g/Fiber 8g
Estimated cost: $9.85

Ingredients:

- Zucchini, 2
- Black pepper, 1 teaspoon
- Shredded cheddar cheese, 1 cup
- Chili powder, 1 teaspoon
- Salt, ½ teaspoon
- Olive oil, 2 tablespoons
- Freshly minced cilantro, ½ cup
- Ground beef, 1 pound

Method:

1. Heat your oven to 400 F.
2. Rinse the zucchinis and pat them dry.
3. Cut the zucchinis into two long halves and remove the seeds.
4. Cook the ground beef in the olive oil for ten minutes, breaking it into small pieces as you stir.
5. Stir in the seasonings and keep cooking until all of the liquid is absorbed, about 5 minutes.
6. Grease a rectangular baking dish.
7. Lay the zucchini halves in the baking dish with the inside facing up.
8. Stir 1/3 of the shredded cheese and the minced cilantro into the beef mixture.
9. Place the meat mixture evenly divided into the zucchini halves.
10. Use the leftover of the shredded cheese to cover and bake for 20 minutes.

Tuna Casserole

Total Prep & Cook Time: 35 minutes

Yields: 4 servings

Nutrition facts: Calories 450/Protein 33g/Carbs 5g/Fat 23g/Fiber 12g

Estimated cost: $6.35

Ingredients:

- Grated parmesan cheese, ½ cup
- Green bell pepper, 1 minced
- Butter, 3 tablespoons
- Salt, ½ teaspoon
- Tuna packed in oil, 16 ounces
- Chili powder, 1 teaspoon
- Yellow onion, 1 peeled and minced
- Celery stalks, 6 minced
- Shredded cheddar cheese, 1 cup
- Black pepper, 1 teaspoon
- Mayonnaise, 1 cup

Method:

1. Heat your oven to 400 F.
2. Fry the veggies in the melted butter for 5 minutes, stirring frequently.
3. Mix the mayonnaise, parmesan cheese, chili powder, salt, pepper, and tuna.
4. Grease a 9-inch baking pan.
5. Put the tuna mixture in the baking pan.
6. Sprinkle the mixture of veggies on top of the tuna mixture in the baking dish.
7. Add the leftover shredded cheese on top of the veggie mixture.
8. Bake the tuna casserole for 20 minutes.

Philly Chicken Cheesesteak

Total Prep & Cook Time: 30 minutes
Yields: 3 servings
Nutritional facts: Calories 263/Protein 27g/Carbs 5g/Fat 13g/Fiber 7g
Estimated cost: $5.85

Ingredients:

- Diced green bell pepper, ½ cup
- Worcestershire sauce, 2 tablespoons
- Black pepper, ½ teaspoon
- Minced garlic, 1 teaspoon
- Onion powder, ½ teaspoon
- Provolone cheese, 3 slices
- Olive oil, 2 teaspoons divided
- Garlic powder, ½ teaspoon
- Chicken breast, raw, 2
- Diced white onion, ½ cup

Method:

1. Slice the chicken breasts into ¼ inch thick slices and place them in a bowl for mixing.
2. Add in the onion powder, Worcestershire sauce, garlic powder, and pepper, and toss the chicken pieces to coat them well.
3. Fry the chicken slices in 1 teaspoon of the olive oil for 10 minutes, stirring often.
4. Take the chicken out and drain.
5. Fry the bell pepper, onion, and garlic in the other teaspoon of olive oil for 4 minutes.
6. Stir the chicken into the veggies to blend, and then turn off the heat.
7. Separate the mixture into three serving bowls and lay one slice of cheese on top of each bowl.

Spinach Salmon Burgers

Total Prep & Cook Time: 40 minutes
Yields: 4 servings
Nutritional facts: Calories 224/Protein 12g/Carbs 2g/Fat 9g/Fiber 6g
Estimated cost: $8.35

Ingredients:

- Diced onion, ¼ cup
- Sour cream, 2 tablespoons
- Mayonnaise, ¼ cup
- Freshly chopped dill, 1 tablespoon
- Chopped spinach, ½ cup
- Ground flax, 1 tablespoon
- Canned salmon, 1 16-ounce can
- Lemon juice, 1 tablespoon
- Sliced mozzarella cheese, 4
- Coconut oil, 2 tablespoon
- Egg, 1
- Keto flatbread, 4 slices

Method:

1. Blend the spinach, egg, sour cream, and lemon juice.
2. Stir in the chopped dill, onion, and flax meal.
3. Form this mixture into four patties of equal size.
4. Fry the patties in coconut oil for 5 minutes for each side.
5. Serve the patties on a slice of keto flatbread with mayonnaise as needed.

6.3 Dinner Recipes

Pork Chops with Kale and Bacon Pesto

Total Prep & Cook Time: 1 hour
Yields: 6 servings
Nutritional facts: Calories 379/Protein 44g/Carbs 9g/Fat 40g/Fiber 4g
Estimated cost: $10.25

Ingredients:

- Crushed pork rind, 1 cup
- Fresh chopped basil, 1 cup
- Minced garlic, 2 tablespoons
- Black pepper, 1 teaspoon
- Shredded cheddar cheese, ½ cup
- Egg, 1
- Salt, ½ teaspoon
- Dried oregano, 1 teaspoon
- Olive oil, ¼ cup
- Turmeric, 1 teaspoon
- Almond milk, ¼ cup
- Baby kale, 2 cups
- Pork chops, 6 thin cut and boneless
- Minced walnuts, ½ cup
- Crisp cooked bacon, 4 slices

Method:

1. Heat your oven to 350 F.
2. Use grease to coat a rectangular baking dish.
3. Whip the milk into the egg.
4. In a shallow bowl, blend the crushed pork rind, shredded cheese, oregano, pepper, and salt.

5. Put the pork chops in the crumbs, then into the egg mixture, and again in the crumb mixture.
6. Lay the coated pork chops in the greased baking dish and bake them for 35 minutes, turning the chops after 20 minutes.
7. While the chops are baking, blend the kale with the olive oil, garlic, basil, walnuts, and crumbled bacon to make the pesto.
8. Serve the creamy kale pesto with the pork chops.

Almond and Artichoke Chicken Breasts

Total Prep & Cook Time: 85 minutes
Yields: 4 servings
Nutritional facts: Calories 350/Protein 26g/Carbs 7g/Fat 12g/Fiber 9g
Estimated cost: $8.95

Ingredients:

- Black pepper, 1 teaspoon
- Artichoke hearts, 1 can
- Chopped roasted almonds, 2 tablespoons
- Chopped baby spinach, ½ cup
- Chicken breast, skinless and boneless, 4
- Salt, ½ teaspoon
- Grated parmesan cheese, 2 tablespoons
- Olive oil, 2 tablespoons
- Cumin, 1 teaspoon

Method:

1. Mix the spinach, almonds, artichoke hearts, parmesan cheese, cumin, and half of the pepper and salt in a mixing bowl.
2. Cut open one side of each chicken breast to create a pocket. Do not slice all the way through.
3. Divide the mixture evenly and fill the chicken breasts.
4. Sprinkle the remaining pepper and salt on the chicken breasts.
5. Cook the breasts in olive oil for 10 minutes for each side.

Baked Maple Cod with Broccoli

Total Prep & Cook Time: 40 minutes
Yields: 2 servings
Nutritional facts: Calories 285/Protein 31 g/Carbs 5g/Fat 13g/Fiber 8g
Estimated cost: $8.85

Ingredients:

- Salt, ½ teaspoon
- Poppy seeds, 1 teaspoon
- Chopped onion, ¼ cup
- 4-ounce cod fillets, 2
- Black pepper, ½ teaspoon
- Olive oil, 1 tablespoon
- Garlic powder, 1 teaspoon
- Dijon mustard, 3 tablespoons
- Broccoli florets, 2 cups
- Mustard powder, ¼ teaspoon
- Lemon juice, 1 tablespoon

Method:

1. Heat your oven to 400 F.
2. Blend until smooth and creamy the Dijon mustard, poppy seed, salt, pepper, olive oil, garlic, and mustard powder.
3. Grease a 9-inch baking dish and place the cod fillets in it.
4. Coat the fish with the Dijon mustard mix.
5. Sprinkle the chopped onion on the fish and bake for 25 minutes.
6. Cook the broccoli florets for ten minutes in boiling water.
7. Place the fish and broccoli on serving plates and dribble everything with lemon juice.

Beef Gratin with Brussel Sprouts

Total Prep & Cook Time: 35 minutes
Yields: 4 servings
Nutritional facts: Calories 750/Protein 40g/Carbs 7g/Fat 59g/Fiber 6g
Estimated cost: $10.25

Ingredients:

- Sour cream, 4 tablespoons
- Italian seasoning, 1 tablespoon
- Ground beef, 1 pound
- Black pepper, 1 teaspoon
- Olive oil, 2 tablespoons
- Dried thyme, ½ teaspoon
- Ground cumin, 1 teaspoon
- Shredded cheddar cheese, 1 cup
- Brussel sprouts, two cups sliced in half
- Chopped parsley, 1 tablespoon
- Salt, 1 teaspoon

Method:

1. Heat your oven to 400 F.
2. Brown, the Brussel sprouts halves for 5 minutes, stirring frequently.
3. Add the sour cream to the Brussel sprouts and mix well and remove from the heat.
4. Grease an eight-inch baking dish.
5. Pour the sprouts and cream into the baking dish.
6. Pepper and salt the meat and brown, often stirring, for about 8 to 10 minutes.
7. Pour the beef on top of the sprout mixture.
8. Blend the Italian seasoning, thyme, cumin, and parsley and sprinkle this over the beef mixture.

9. Spread shredded cheese on the meat and bake the casserole for twenty minutes.

Cuban Style Chicken and Vegetables

Total Prep & Cook Time: 85 minutes
Yields: 4 servings
Nutritional facts: Calories 375/Protein 28g/Carbs 5g/Fat 16g/Fiber 10g
Estimated cost: $9.45

Ingredients:

- Balsamic vinegar, ½ cup
- Chicken legs, 8
- Avocado oil, 1 teaspoon
- Lime juice, ¼ cup
- Salt, ½ teaspoon
- Minced garlic, 2 teaspoons
- Ground cumin, 2 teaspoons
- Black pepper, 1 teaspoon
- Chopped cilantro, ½ cup
- Chunked butternut squash, 2 cups
- Dried oregano, 2 teaspoons
- Green bell pepper, 1 cleaned and sliced

Method:

1. Heat your oven to 500 F.
2. Grease a rectangular baking dish.
3. Place the chicken legs in the baking dish and season.
4. Arrange the pepper slices and squash chunks around the chicken legs in the baking dish.
5. Stir the balsamic vinegar, lime juice, garlic, oregano, avocado oil, cumin, and cilantro in a bowl.
6. Pour the lime juice mixture over the ingredients in the baking dish and bake uncovered for 1 hour.

Pork Chops with Blueberry Sauce

Total Prep & Cook Time: 30 minutes

Yields: 2 servings

Nutritional facts: Calories 310/Protein 21g/Carbs 3g/Fat 9g/Fiber 3g

Estimated cost: $7.45

Ingredients:

- Diced shallot, 1
- Black pepper, ½ teaspoon
- Boneless pork chops, 4
- Lemon juice, 2 tablespoons
- Salt, ½ teaspoon
- Olive oil, 2 tablespoons
- Fresh or frozen blueberries, ½ cup
- Water, ¼ cup
- Chopped fresh parsley, ¼ cup

Method:

1. Heat your oven to 425 F.
2. Pepper and salt the pork chops.
3. Fry the pork chops in 1 tablespoon of the oil for five minutes for each side.
4. Grease a rectangular baking pan and put the chops in it.
5. Bake the chops for 15 minutes.
6. While the chops are baking, fry the shallots for 4 minutes in the other tablespoon of olive oil.
7. Put the lemon juice, blueberries, and water into the skillet.
8. Cook for 3 to 5 more minutes, constantly stirring while the mixture becomes thick.
9. Serve the blueberry sauce with the pork chops.

Macaroni and Cheese

Total Prep & Cook Time: 25 minutes
Yields: 4 servings
Nutritional facts: Calories 314/Protein 11g/Carbs 7g/Fat 23g/Fiber 3g
Estimated cost: $5.25

Ingredients:

- Butter, 3 tablespoons divided
- Black pepper, ½ teaspoon
- Shredded cheddar cheese, 1 cup
- Unsweetened almond milk, ¼ cup
- Salt, ½ teaspoon
- Heavy cream, ¼ cup
- Cauliflower, 1 head chopped into florets

Method:

1. Heat your oven to 450 F.
2. Grease a medium-sized baking sheet.
3. Melt two tablespoons of the butter and pour it over the cauliflower florets in a mixing bowl, tossing them gently to coat.
4. Put the cauliflower on the cookie pan in one layer and bake them for fifteen minutes.
5. Place the leftover butter in a pan with the heavy cream and almond milk while the florets are baking.
6. Stir while heating the milk mixture until it is smooth and creamy.
7. Blend the cheese sauce with the roasted cauliflower florets and mix well.

Basil Tomato Poached Fish

Total Prep & Cook Time: 45 minutes

Yields: 4 servings

Nutritional facts: Calories 245/Protein 34g/Carbs 5g/Fat 2g/Fiber 3g

Estimated cost: $8.25

Ingredients:

- Freshly chopped basil leaves, ¼ cup
- 6-ounce whitefish fillets, 4
- Black pepper, ½ teaspoon
- Olive oil, 2 tablespoons
- Salt, ½ teaspoon
- Dried rosemary, ½ teaspoon
- Vegetable broth, ¾ cup
- Minced garlic, 1 tablespoon
- Dried parsley, 1 teaspoon
- Cherry tomatoes, 2 cups sliced in half

Method:

1. Fry the tomatoes, salt, pepper, parsley, rosemary, and garlic in the oil for five minutes, stirring occasionally.
2. Mix in the chopped basil and broth and blend well.
3. Lay the fish fillets in the skillet.
4. Simmer the fish in a covered skillet for 25 minutes.
5. Serve with a leafy green salad.

Sesame Chicken

Total Prep & Cook Time: 30 minutes

Yields: 2 servings

Nutritional facts: Calories 520/Protein 45g/Carbs 4g/Fat 36g/Fiber 5g

Estimated cost: $9.25

Ingredients:

- FOR THE CHICKEN
    - Egg, 1
    - Salt, ¼ teaspoon
    - Boneless skinless chicken thighs, 1 pound cubed
    - Arrowroot powder, 1 tablespoon
    - Black pepper, ½ teaspoon
    - Toasted sesame seed oil, 1 tablespoon

- FOR THE SAUCE
    - Ground ginger, 1 tablespoon
    - Toasted sesame seed oil, 1 tablespoon
    - Chopped green onion, ¼ cup
    - Xanthan gum, ¼ teaspoon
    - Broccoli florets, 1 cup
    - Vinegar, 1 tablespoon
    - Sesame seeds, 4 tablespoons
    - Soy sauce, 3 tablespoons
    - Minced garlic, 2 tablespoon

Method:

1. Blend the egg and arrowroot powder.
2. Coat the chicken chunks with the egg mixture.
3. Fry the coated chicken in 1 tablespoon of toasted sesame oil, turning gently for ten minutes.
4. While the thigh chunks are frying, blend the sauce ingredients until they are smooth and creamy.

5. Boil the florets for 5 minutes.
6. Put the sauce on the chicken and cook for five more minutes, often stirring while the sauce thickens.
7. Drop the chicken in a serving bowl and toss with the cooked broccoli florets.
8. Dribble the chopped green onion over the top and serve.

Lime Coconut Skirt Steak

Total Prep & Cook Time: 40 minutes
Yields: 4 servings
Nutrition facts: Calories 661/Protein 35g/Carbs 5g/Fat 54g/Fiber 0g
Estimated cost: $11.50

Ingredients:

- Ground ginger, 1 teaspoon
- Red pepper flakes, 1 teaspoon
- Lime zest, 1 tablespoon
- Coconut oil, ½ cup
- Salt, ½ teaspoon
- Minced garlic, 1 tablespoon
- Lime juice, 2 tablespoons
- Skirt steak, 2 pounds

Method:

1. Blend the lime juice, red pepper flakes, melted coconut oil, lime zest, salt, ginger, and garlic.
2. Cover all of the steaks with the lime juice mixture.
3. Let the steaks rest for twenty minutes at room temperature.
4. Sear the steaks on both sides for 30 seconds per side in a hot, dry skillet.
5. Fry the steaks for five minutes on each side over medium heat.
6. Slice against the grain to serve.

6.4 Dessert Recipes

Dessert is allowed on the keto diet, as long as you eat the right kind of dessert. Try these desserts and see just how good keto eating can be.

Cheesecake Fat Bombs

Total Prep & Cook Time: 140 minutes
Yields: 24 bombs
Nutrition facts: Calories 103/Protein 2g/Carbs 2g/Fat 10g/Fiber 1g
Estimated cost: $3.75

Ingredients:

- Xylitol, 2 tablespoons
- Cream cheese, four ounces softened to room temperature
- Creamy peanut butter, ¼ cup
- Unsweetened dark chocolate chips, mini-sized, ½ cup

Method:

1. Cream the cream cheese, xylitol, and peanut butter until everything is smooth.
2. Form the mixture into mini-balls about one inch thick and roll them in the mini chocolate chips.
3. Set the fat bombs on a plate covered in wax paper and freeze them for 2 hours.
4. Store the fat bombs covered in the refrigerator.

Speedy Brownies

Total Prep & Cook Time: 25 minutes
Yields: 9 brownies
Nutrition facts: Calories 129/Protein 3g/Carbs 3g/Fat 4g/Fiber 2g
Estimated cost: $3.50

Ingredients:

- Cocoa powder, 1 tablespoon
- Chocolate protein powder, 1 scoop
- Unsweetened dark chocolate chips, 2 tablespoons
- Stevia, 1 tablespoon
- Almond milk, ¼ cup
- Coconut Flour, 1 tablespoon
- Baking powder, ½ teaspoon
- Egg, 1

Method:

1. Heat your oven to 340 F.
2. Grease a nine-inch baking dish.
3. Mix the cocoa powder, coconut flour, stevia, baking powder, and protein powder.
4. Stir in the milk, egg, and chocolate chips.
5. Put the batter into the baking dish and bake for fifteen minutes.

Churn Free Ice Cream

Total Prep & Cook Time: 7 hours
Yields: ½ gallon
Nutrition facts per ½ cup prepared: Calories 345/Protein 2g/Carbs 2g/Fat 36g/Fiber 1g
Estimated cost: $5.15

Ingredients:

- Xylitol, 1/3 cup
- Coconut oil, ½ cup
- Heavy cream, 3 cups divided
- Vanilla extract, 1 teaspoon
- Butter, 3 tablespoons

Method:

1. Melt the butter.
2. Blend in the xylitol with 2 cups of the heavy cream.
3. Boil this mixture.
4. Lessen the heat and cook the mixture for 30 to 45 minutes, so it becomes thick.
5. Put the mixture into a large bowl and leave it to adjust to room temperature.
6. Add in the coconut oil and vanilla extract.
7. In a different bowl, whip one cup of cream to stiff peaks.
8. Slowly fold the whipped cream into the boiled cream.
9. Scoop the mixture into a bowl that is safe for the freezer.
10. Freeze for at least 6 hours.

Orange Cake Bites

Total Prep & Cook Time: 20 minutes
Yields: 15 cake balls
Nutrition facts per cake ball: Calories 92/Protein 3g/Carbs 4g/Fat 7g/Fiber 2g
Estimated cost: $5.20

Ingredients:

- Orange zest, 2 tablespoons
- Cinnamon, 1 teaspoon
- Coconut flour, 1/3 cup
- Vanilla extract, ½ teaspoon
- Almond butter, 2/3 cup
- Stevia, ¼ cup
- Unsweetened orange juice, ¼ cup

Method:

1. Blend everything in a mixing bowl until the batter is creamy.
2. Form 15 balls from the cake mixture.
3. Lightly roll each cake ball into a small amount of coconut flour. Freeze the cake balls for 10 minutes to chill them.

Lemon Bars

Total Prep & Cook Time: 60 minutes

Yields: 8 servings

Nutrition facts: Calories 272/Protein 8g/Carbs 4g/Fat 26g/Fiber 5g

Estimated cost: $4.85

Ingredients:

- Eggs, 3 large
- Lemons, 3 medium-sized
- Powdered erythritol, 1 cup divided
- Almond flour, 1 ¾ cup divided
- Butter, ½ cup melted

Method:

1. Cream together one cup of almond flour, the butter, and ¼ cup of the erythritol.
2. Cover an eight-inch baking pan with parchment paper.
3. Press the almond flour mixture onto the parchment paper.
4. Juice the lemons and zest one.
5. Add a three-fourths cup of almond flour with the zest and juice, eggs, and three-fourths cup of erythritol and stir well.
6. Put the mixture in the baking dish.
7. Bake the bars for 25 minutes.

Pumpkin Cheesecake Mousse

Total Prep & Cook Time: 15 minutes
Yields: 10 servings
Nutrition facts per ½ cup serving: Calories 215/Protein 3g/Carbs 3g/Fat 18g/Fiber 1g
Estimated cost: $5.85

Ingredients:

- Pumpkin pie spice, 2 tablespoons
- Vanilla extract, 2 teaspoons
- Powdered erythritol, ½ cup
- Unsweetened pumpkin puree, 1 15-ounce can
- Cream cheese, 12 ounces softened to room temperature
- Heavy cream, ¾ cup

Method:

1. Cream the pumpkin puree and the cream cheese until smooth and creamy.
2. Blend in the heavy cream, pumpkin pie spice, vanilla extract, and erythritol until well mixed.
3. Keep in the refrigerator for at least 1 hour before serving.

Peanut Butter Blondies

Total Prep & Cook Time: 35 minutes

Yields: 9 pieces

Nutrition facts: Calories 103/Protein 3g/Carbs 1g/Fat 9g/Fiber 2g

Estimated cost: $5.85

Ingredients:

- Almond flour, ¼ cup
- Butter, 4 tablespoons softened to room temperature
- Stevia, ¼ cup
- Melted raw cocoa butter, 3 tablespoons
- Creamy peanut butter, ½ cup
- Eggs, 2
- Vanilla extract, 1 teaspoon

Method:

1. Heat your oven to 350.
2. Grease a nine-inch baking pan.
3. Blend the vanilla extract, eggs, butter, peanut butter, and raw cocoa butter until smooth.
4. Put in the flour and mix.
5. Bake for twenty-five minutes.
6. Let the bars cool for at least 2 hours before slicing.

Chocolate Frosty Dessert

Total Prep & Cook Time: 1 hour
Yields: 2 servings
Nutrition facts: Calories 241/Protein 3g/Carbs 4g/Fat 25g/Fiber 0g
Estimated cost: $4.75

Ingredients:

- Salt, 1 pinch
- Heavy whipping cream, 1 ½ cup
- Unsweetened cocoa powder, 2 tablespoons
- Powdered erythritol, 3 tablespoons
- Vanilla extract, 1 teaspoon

Method:

1. Cream the heavy cream, salt, sweetener, cocoa powder, and vanilla until the mixture forms stiff peaks.
2. Freeze the mixture for 45 minutes before serving.

Blueberry Cupcakes

Total Prep & Cook Time: 30 minutes

Yields: 12 servings

Nutrition facts: Calories 138/Protein 5g/Carbs 5g/Fat 12g/fiber 2g

Estimated cost: $6.10

Ingredients:

- Coconut flour, ½ cup
- Lemon zest, 2 tablespoons
- Vanilla extract, 1 teaspoon
- Eggs, 8
- Lemon juice, 2 tablespoons
- Stevia, 4 tablespoons
- Baking powder, 1 teaspoon
- Fresh blueberries, 1 cup
- Butter, 1 stick melted

Method:

1. Heat your oven to 350 F.
2. Blend the lemon zest, lemon juice, vanilla, baking powder, coconut flour, sweetener, and melted butter.
3. Put in the eggs and blend well.
4. Place cupcake papers in all 12 cups of a muffin pan, then spray with spray oil.
5. Fill the cupcake papers evenly.
6. Set several blueberries into the batter of each cupcake.
7. Bake the cupcakes for 15 minutes.
8. Blend cream cheese with lemon juice to make frosting for the cupcakes.

Conclusion

Thank you for your decision to purchase *Keto Cookbook for Men*. Hopefully, you found the book loaded with useful information and enjoyable for you, and that you now have all the information you will need to attain your goals, whatever they may be.

The next step is to begin your change to the keto lifestyle, using the ideas and recipes found in this book to start your journey. The keto lifestyle is the answer you have been seeking; the plan will restore your good health while enabling you to lose weight and feel great. Keto eating is not dull, as the recipes in this book will prove. They provide a good idea of how you will now be eating for the remainder of your life. These recipes will also give your ideas for creating your keto meals and menus.

As you have seen by the recipes in this book, keto is not so restrictive that you will not enjoy delicious food while losing weight and feeling great. It is so much easier to stick with an eating plan full of foods you want to eat, and the keto lifestyle gives you this ability. Do not be afraid to try new dishes that might seem strange to you because you might find a new favorite among all of the possibilities out there.

One final note -- if *Keto Cookbook for Men* proved to be useful for you in any way, a review on Amazon is appreciated!

Tables

Abbreviations

Milliliter	**ml**
Liter	l
Gallon	gal
Quart	qt
Pint	pt
Cup	cup
Fluid Ounce	fl oz
Tablespoon	tbsp
Teaspoon	tsp
Dessertspoon	dstpsn
Kilogram	kg
Gram	g
Pounds	lb
Ounces	oz
Celsius	C
Fahrenheit	F

Conversion

Measure	Fluid OZ	TBSP	TSP	Liter/milliliter
1 gallon	4 qt	256 tbsp	768 tsp	3.8 l
4 cup	1 qt	64 tbsp	192 tsp	.95 l
2 cup	1 pt	32 tbsp	96 tsp	470 ml
1 cup	8 oz	16 tbsp	48 tsp	237 ml
3/4 cup	6 oz	12 tbsp	35 tsp	177 ml
2/3 cup	5 oz	11 tbsp	32 tsp	158 ml
1/2 cup	4 oz	8 tbsp	24 tsp	118 ml
1/3 cup	3 oz	5 tbsp	16 tsp	79 ml
1/4 cup	2 oz	4 tbsp	12 tsp	59 ml
1/8 cup	1 oz	2 tbsp	6 tsp	30 ml
1/16 cup	.5 oz	1 tbsp	3 tsp	15 ml

Temperature conversions

Celsius	Fahrenheit
1	33.8
100	212
110	230
120	248
130	266
140	284
150	302

160	320
170	338
180	356
190	374
200	392
210	410
220	428
230	446
240	464
250	482
260	500

Made in the USA
Las Vegas, NV
15 June 2021

24755072R00052